Chiseled Orchids

Also by W.R. Taylor

The Geography of Grief

Published by New Athens Press

Chiseled Orchids

W.R. Taylor

New Athens Press

0 9 8 7 6 5 4 3 2 1

First Paperback Edition

978-1-387-39673-3

Back cover photo "Cowboys, Folsom Street Fair" Copyright © 1995 by Tim Krafft.

Inquiries may be sent to:
NewAthensPress@gmail.com

for A.C.

They are sent whoring into town,

    decked out with nauseating *luxury*.

        —Arthur Rimbaud

Ventriloquist Act

Oil Derricks At Night Under Spotlights

Reference points secure my location
outside his scene
cast in a certain atmosphere of art and violence
burning lines on tinfoil to make it through the night
still afraid to completely mesh
in the recycled gossip of who kicked whose ass
and how much food so-and-so gave me and that awesome trick
who introduced me to his friends we all got really high
partied all night
then this morning when we crashed
he made me sleep on the couch
because that one red patch
on the inside of my leg
won't go away no matter what I do.

Strung Along

i.
Minds so close they actually breathe
each other's thoughts   child pains
longing his touch sober words
not another friend to string out and medicate with—
another stranger you tell your life to
when you're tweaked
     there may have been a time when I needed a father in my life
but I outgrew that   take care of myself now
he's nothing more
     than a consistent score.

ii.
Smokes another line on tinfoil
mocks his knobby naked speed-build
tiny once-pierced nipples
speed-horny   strung out
vaguely numb
masturbated for days pink rubber penis
     takes a while for it to get hard
but then I cum right away.

Lipstick

Blotted on napkins
paper products smudged
her shade   all my life
waste baskets overflow

        Dreams of being her
hands on bureau   stare in mirror
tube poised in air   hummingbird
dabs red   retreats staining
stare again her face   in mine
mother   softened
blended male

        Crush napkin to mouth not blotting
wiping   her eyes
her lips away.

Tenderness Was Lacking

Not because of his mohawk or tattooed vine
of thorny roses over one ear
but because of a familiar hunger
known to us as men
a desperation driven by sex-need
for same-touch;
flat stomachs pressed together
the violence of calloused hands restrained
teeth bared biting knotted neck muscle
—making stone bend.

He touched me like strange meat and not himself
held my cock like it was some plastic
unbreakable toy
—shaking it hard to make it work.

It's A Bastard Gesture

Dodging calls avoiding home
panicked running between cafes to street-guys' eyes
wishing I could move in
to dragging dirty skater pants
black and purple hair
porcelain cup of perfect nostrils
torn canvas hi-tops
    dirt-streaked feet kicking the concrete
every skated step.

This hollow gaze which never fills.

Conversations Of Need

I don't want any part of it of human beings
of the way I feel inside
at the shame I was raised to feel was mine.

Still not knowing what to do with these feelings
sweet longing my hands   a young man's heart
heat and tenderness of pressed skin
    moment my breath catches.

Holding fast to that fragile connection
severed in orgasm.

Manufactured Images No Longer Feed Me

I want sand in my teeth with every cigarette
like deposits left in my lungs after every drag
I want the soft bones of another man in my bed asleep
his skin so hot it keeps me up nights
    —you know I can't sleep when I'm hot.

Abrasion of his leg hair rubbing mine
friction of his pubes when we face each other fucking
mirror slide of astrolube
sticky lips pressed to his neck
and the smell of our breath in the morning
made tangible.

Not these phantoms
memory of another man I don't speak to now
his toes in my mouth which are only my fingers
choking me as I fight collapsing erection

    struggledejection.

Unexpected   A New Man's Taste

Curl of his tongue inside my lips
    having to adjust

Whereas he   used to this pattern
relates out of habit
kisses my knuckles
    tangles my fingers in his   reassuring

Jarring   another body's smell
unexpected touch of his skin
back of my neck   pressed lips
arms settled around my waist
    carelessly
absent that pressing need

Solid cock which hints at violence
presses my ass   minus the impatient
breath of rape

Smell of shit on his fingertips
sticky-sweet of lubricant   shine
spirals up my shaft to the head
automatic hands tear open a condom
pulls out the second he sees me wince
    I'm sorry
I thought it's what you wanted.

Ventriloquist Act

His hand wrapped around my spine
snaps head to attention
jaw muscles clench
his desolate voice
consumes my own.

Watch him think, listen as
his ugly, dispassionate intellect
cracks my faded pink lips
with lies like
suffering makes pure.

Voiceless screaming block of wood.

A Ron Athey Performance

I couldn't dance hard enough afterwards
sadness overwhelming like the letdown after sex
only worse
everyone around me applauded
symbolic rape enacted on stage
three white men attacking single black stripper
man beside me yelled   *Make her bleed.*

Puppet Show (16th & Mission)

Cradled her wound like a newborn, nursing bitterness. Yellow eyes
hostile longing. Strings taut, skin knotted.

Outfits! Outfits! Limped by on syringe crutches,
pursued by cigarette smoke.

Eddie Discovers Gravity

I felt my innocence a house of cards collapse the syringe on Shiva's desk
a dirty spoon pyrex glass measure half filled
another glass of dirty water beside it Eddie nodded
his sunflower face following the sun
head thrown back the perfect line
up his neck Adam's apple ridge dimpled chin
open-mouthed gray lips perfect teeth slowly pulsing sponge tongue
aquiline nose eye-slits wavy brown tendriled hair
falling with gravity hungry for his mouth
desire time
when he nods completely
hesitant fingertips
trace ripple along his ribs
he notices from somewhere
but cannot care.

Fire Clay

Tim will be forgotten, another casualty
caught short, prior to recognition
his alarm clock forever sounding 7:30am.
His strained breathing through our shared
bedroom wall holding me from precipice of sleep.

Hands clasped behind his head
sleeping off a drunk I thought
wouldn't awaken. Shut off his clock.
Glasses off, partially awake
I saw no needle on his bedroom floor
no stained water or carbonized spoon.

Leaving for work, paused at his door
his jagged snore was silent. My failure to pry,
failed to preserve that expansive, playful mind
from a junkie's death. There are no experiments
with heroin, the wish to dissolve
into pleasure a lilac suicide. Tim
should have been more than a casualty

Worrying my dreams for years after
I emptied our apartment
rolled his change jar quarters
for pizza, spackled puncture-speckled dart board walls
erased our lives from that San Francisco apartment
of bagels, clowns, kites and Gertrude Stein
indelibly memorized.

Spinneret's Made Mainly Of Gold

Our fallen bayou prince Eddie smiled, his eyes
squinting through dreamy opiate haze,
called me "Pure" the morning
of Tim's funeral. His beautiful mouth
caressed the word as if to entice me
to join him in the authenticity
of addiction. Bygone nobility
idly painting somnolent erotic fantasies
with syringe paintbrushes
bought by trust funds. But I
caught the price: every fatal overdose
he presided over ensured his immortality;
blood prick thirst quench paralysis death —forever
rich and beautiful. He intended
me to be his next. Doggedly impure,
angered by his mawkish suggestion
I rebelled with an expletive, shocking him
out of his drowsy seduction
ending my brief flirtation with heroin.

Leather Rusting

His jacket fell there by the chair
and I stooped to pick it up
bringing it to my lips, my hands
delighting in the feel
of tired leather worn down to his fragile size.

Inhale and remember bacon frying on Sundays following long
drinking nights, cloying nausea
still writhing on the inner sea.

—There cleaves his cigarettes
like cologne strong and sad
but stronger still for nights consumed in nervous fingers
caught out in the rain
alone in his lonely arms
hugging his chest
afraid to fall
—black rusting cycle leaning heavy against the wind
and coffee stops at roadsides
when there was no money for beer.

I pull his jacket over me
fold myself into wooden kitchen chair.

Syncopations II.

Barstow Kelly adopted Craig at fourteen
       willowy, awkward teenage gay boy
             now spins records in a San Francisco basement
             hosts a new guy every night
     in nowhere California town
a queen bee nurtures her own.

Braille Typewriters

His touch provokes a flow of words
adjectives strung together in random order
murmured watercolor sketch of pleasure
at cool fingertips that trace
shoulder mounds of scar tissue
shudders delighted, unbroken lines
that disappear the moment they're spoken.

Chance Encounter

Teach me the spirit of this time
manners and slights
customs that changed
somewhere between
amphetamine disco seventies
and the Epidemic. Teach me to hope
that in my fragile seed of hearts
protected by its apricot stone sheath
that unreturned phone calls
like expired lottery tickets
count for nothing;
that a surprise smile on the street
like a renewed promise
or answered prayer
can dispel this caustic loneliness
and restore the balance of hope. These ocean tides
of unending struggle, crash
withdrawal and resurgence
made up of millions of gold flecks
salt and sewage.

Love Too Easily

Don't give me that smile, I see through
your young Chet Baker looks, style
evoking the way he covered his bases and sang
he'd never been in love, "don't change
a hair for me," then regretfully
"the thrill is gone." You've got it too
the coy pretender, that wicked smile—
you've been here before —the shy suitor.
Who played the reticent love
the last time you acted this scene?
Who will play it next? Will you seek
a companion easy in ecstasy, confident
among strangers, whose perfect skin
erases my flawed; whose glassy mind
dispels this fractured piece; whose
sexual poise reflects our nervous time
as lacking? I can't stand to try. Not
tonight. I take your casual sidewalk smile
and immediately glance away.

Mama's Mascara *Runs*, Honey

When we drink we miss those nights when hookers dabbed blood
off our crooked, grin-split faces
and offered to pave over the bruises with foundation
for a cigarette and how Finessa Cruella
pinched my ass and played
Liz Taylor, sneered "What a Dump."
Palms up, hands making wide, victorious arcs.

We Live Like We're In A Party

Designer clothes strike
defiant poses

every cocktail laugh
a silken blade of derision

impatient to walk away
the moment we're bored.

Monique's True Father By Way of Nico and
        That Delinquent Queerboy Rimbaud

We all wanted to bear Jim Morrison's offspring
the guys in the crowd somehow wanting it most of all.

An Athena in horsehide leather jacket sprung fully-formed
composed in a Helmet of War.

An owl familiar perched on one solid shoulder.

Utterly tremendous in a fantastic fucking semi-frocked Blade Runner
disguise.

Pact

Rode in the back of the truck, drunk with Seamus, staring at steel supports of Bay Bridge making pacts. Will, dammit. This is serious. Let's be young forever. Alright. Gripped hands, wheeling stars in black night. Flash of passing bridge lights. Slug of vodka.

Subbacultcha

Rhythmic hum of tires on asphalt interstate
muscle car bass-line of early Pixies, Black Francis'
dry delivery, half-speaking on this orange-tinted,
harvest moon night. Dye-black bangs
get in eyes, brushed aside sleeve of lime
green bowling shirt, small-town league
lettered across the back. Aimed at Santa Fe
rich hippie friends in weird New Age mansions
spinning wax to the Infinite, sipping bottled water
pissing clear. Hot chai lattes at daybreak
all the pancakes you can eat smothered in soy butter
and that sweet guy from Burning Man
with the laughing smile and dusty bare feet
who shared a joke and opened my eyes.

Kit Fox

You got that smile low to the ground, that sandy grin
running all the way up into your reddish brown fur
close-cropped behind your ears, untamed
tongue hung out in greeting.
I've known you before, the thin limbs
the laughing grace, there's something familiar
I can't quite place it, new to this landscape
dragging the ghosts of the city behind me.
You're quick, but now you approach
with casual languor, pausing at the counter
for an iced coffee, acting almost bored
in your nonchalance, like a coyote
asking tourists for potato chips along the roads
inside the park —that tilt of the head
hungry, but unwilling to show it.
I've got your number, and can't help grinning in reply.

Cowboy Butch

When steam trays of midnight taquerias
lie empty, already wiped down
with damp white towels
when street cars expel
Financial District workaholics
bars overflow onto amber streets
with exhausted smokers
nursing their final rounds
I'll see you in leather brim-crushed
cowboy hat rolled like a wink
above your tomboy grin
arm settled around the waist
of your girl, world at bay
beyond reach of your swinging arm.
We share our scars, worship bruises
bite marks and motorbikes
—and those nights when hard-eyed
hurting brings me in for pizza
you ask no questions but slip me a soda
always glad to see me.

Supple Invocation

Eyes wide, back arched
pleasure that erupts and erases
flashes through miles of nerve fiber
stares his lover's face
then into space
holiness crackles
singes the air.

Candy Says

Candy says
I finally love my body
after all the surgery
has been done.

Candy says
you know it's never easy
to undo your gender slavery
and be free.

Peet's

It's not the first time
I've crushed
on an illusion
wrapped around a pretty guy.

Such Eyes

Such eyes I've only seen on a model, such hard
cold, fish-like eyes, staring back like a wounded
flapping suffocating trout, hooked by the jaw
with the promise of an easy pay off; just remove
your shirt, slowly show
your lean body, remove
your pants, expose
your curved, hardened dick
and we will broadcast your image into eternity
to the lonely, the horny, the purveyors of fleeting beauty
who evaluate your sneer
and admire your eyes
your hardened, fish-like aquarium eyes
trapped in the narrow tank, unable to turn away.

Echo Location

Pale yellow ferns turn, antenna
of some night creature
highly attuned
to dips in the atmosphere. Over drinks
at Bliss Bar I watched you descend
and become hostile;
I was no longer entertaining,
not drinking fast enough
to outpace your cruelty. Panicked
dizzy, I fled outside
to dance among the cigarette lights.

Queen Vets

Our days marked by disappointment
we didn't find Eden via dehydration
dropping E left us weary, down-hearted
every weekend aimed at holy
trying to forget thrift store jobs
and Starbucks
pulling shots hour after hour.
Some wonderland. We count our casualties
on both fists —heroin, K, amphetamine;
we hide their snapshots in shoeboxes
Tim flying kites at Ocean Beach
—dead since '95. We're the lucky ones
who smoked Shermans and laughed with contempt
at summer tides of fresh-faced boys
to be rolled on tongues, in arms, trod underfoot
then gone, either émigrés
or casualties. Some part of us
dead with their loss. And nothing helps
to forget.

Dancing Indoors

One year it was granny glasses
perched on fancy dancer noses
ingeniously secured against drops;
another year, brilliant scarves
woven like perfume of flashy dance regalia;
beautifully beaded sneakers
smiles of admiration
brilliant innovation for indoor dances
held in gymnasium basketball courts
with hard, unforgiving floors; and for me
my lover's teasing smile
as we danced the Circle
the length of a single intertribal song.

Mr. Bungle

Swinging from the mirror ball noose
dancing marionettes jerk on the rope
calliope beats and screaming divas
shirtless corpses twist in the wind
round about, reaching out
such grimaces on their pretty faces
such hunger in their rolling eyes.

Siddhartha

It is snowing in Albuquerque as I dream
your face, your tight lithe body
quivering with masculine energy
pent-up, pushing me away. My landlord's dog
barks at the snowflakes, an obnoxious
Pomeranian ankle biter, and I dream
of cigarettes shared in the doorway of your café
your conscientious rag wiping down tables
your smile at a cassette tape of techno
Herman Hesse in your back pocket, reading
Siddhartha in San Francisco that winter
sneaking quarters into your tip jar, and praying
I could hold you, holding on
to my slipping sanity, with nothing but grief
to offer you, just heartache and desire.
I shiver, the snow falls, and I miss you.

Your Brand

You twist my sheets in thorny vines, haunt my dreams
plague my days, I shudder with longing and smoke your brand
just to be close to you. After a couple drinks the phone in reach
your number leaps to mind unwanted, but I don't dare
this obsession a trap, a mire, a jail.

Look Good, Feel Better

Carol Channing in a size fourteen pump, dancer's thigh
flashing from beneath an emerald evening gown's slit
lip-syncing a chirpy Doris Day ditty about hopeless men
and the trouble with loving them. Loren is drinking a Zombie,
I order the same, glad I came. A cowgirl gets onstage
puckers glossy bubblegum lips to a campy country song, booted swagger
offstage to mingle with the audience, accepting dollar bills
graciously, as hooting gay boys and baby dykes tuck them
into her denim Daisy-Dukes. Tonight all tips go to women with cancer
for wigs and make-up, a "Look Good, Feel Better" fundraiser
organized by Loren as an Initiate into the Sisters
of Perpetual Indulgence, one of only two women in the Order. An ugly novice
totters towards the stage on chunky heels, her mini skirt stretched
like a shrieking trampoline across her ass, performs a teary torch song
hammers fists on table for emphasis, spilling a round of drinks
fatally embarrassed, she doesn't quit, she finishes her song
as wiser, kinder queens than me slip folded bills into her ample cleavage
with loving, generous smiles. Later, when she wins the wig raffle
we all burst into enthusiastic applause.

Homocore Punk, Former Roommate, Lost Boy

Hard-eyed with exhaustion under argon lights and cathode-rays
impatient at the bus stop in a black trench coat
limited protection from the intermittent rain

eyes flicking up Castro to where my bus will eventually crest the hill
then to the steps down to the underground metro station
as another crowded train disgorges more weary workers
I recognize a face, and ache at his accelerating decline.

Lurid hair-dye faded from a top knot lonely on his close-shaved blond head
mouth that never opens to smile its missing teeth; not sure how lost
but knowing he's unable to keep his trap shut
when bullied or threatened.

I nod in recognition, he starts at my ghost
haunted by our briefly shared past
when he lived with his IWW labor organizer boyfriend
in an Outer Mission flat
and offered me the empty room after my roommate's overdose left me
homeless.

Eric.

What were you doing at 3 am practicing your keyboards
when I had to be up at six for work?
My repeated, exhausted pleas to turn the volume down
as you and your friend fresh from rehab
reminisced about getting high.

Oh Eric, I've watched your decline
tried to honor your dignity when I saw you on the street
so proud when you first got clean, got off heroin and got a regular job
serving coffee.
then began to worry as neglected, clumped mascara circled around
angry eyes assigning blame for getting moved to a store
in a less tony neighborhood
on schedule conflicts, and not your escalating inconsistency.

Tonight you hide your eyes from mine, tuck your head
I know you're high
and I'm not ashamed. But I will worry
because I don't want you to die.

Homeless under another ugly night, you disappear
until I'm seated on the bus
then slip aboard, not quite invisible
bob your head while locating me
then hide your face seeking an open seat
far from my gaze, as I stretch my legs in the back
and try to respect your avoidance.

Don't be embarrassed, sweetie. I sympathize with relapse
it's hard to shake a habit as ingrained as self-hate.
Weeks later, I still wish I'd intervened. Sought you out
while waiting at the bus stop. Reassured and encouraged you.

Eric, Do you know me?
Then know this:

Know that you are beautiful inside, and that the injuries done to you
Heal a little more every time you show genuine love to yourself.

How They Make Prostitutes

Teen boy on the street, streaky black hair smoking outside
the bar my queer-male-sister Michel dared me inside,
noted my glance as I passed by.
I ordered our cocktails, anxious and needing a sedative
Sister just as cool as anything standing there like a bitter pillar
carved from the harshest salts picked a table in the center
up against the wall opposite the bar that stretched nearly the length
of that long over-lit room. Michel decided to have a smoke
I watched the rough trade leaning over the pool table
and posing with their cues. A sturdy blond who could take care of himself
detached himself from the game to hi. "Just watching the game."
I smiled at him. He shrugged *your loss* and turned around.

Michel returned, thrusting his shoulders forward, pivoting at the waist,
his torso a shadowy 'v' that cut into his tight black 't'
faded charcoal same as his slacks, wearing his buckled "little girl shoes".
He took his seat with a dirty grin and noted my eyes
return to the doorway to watch the morbid waif from outside
shuffle back into the bar. My eyes noticed too long. He made a beeline
to our table and mumbling, tried to ingratiate. I gulped my Stoli-tonic.
I asked his story. It's the same story.
Every story the same story no matter what's said, by whom, any gender
it doesn't matter because why never changes. The pitch is everything
especially when unrehearsed. Not a thief. Honest. Always
make good on deals. Never freaked out. Not lying.
I told him we were tourists, not voyeurs. That I wasn't there to use anyone.
"I'm not about using anybody either." He corrected me with wary,
resentful eyes. But we were just checking out the bar.
"At least you weren't a-huggin' and kissin' on me before you said so."

Glass Cages

> I am a glass human disappearing in rain.
> —David Wojnarowicz

This translucent skin, cables of blood
and muscle coiled beneath
flex, relax and strain
with an exertion of pointless extremity
what's it all for really? One wonders
hesitates then quits. Just continue
ask the questions but keep on.
The rain falls, the skeleton struggles
to mount gravity and stand
the neon signs of this society go out in segments
never replaced or repaired
as long as some flicker of hot pink light
reaches consumers eager to escape the rain
of desire, the pleasures of this thin skin
rippling under glass.

Moscow / St. Petersburg

А такому,
как я,
Ткнуться куда?
Где для меня уготовано логово?"

—*В. Маяковский, (1916)*

Moscow / St. Petersburg

i. Beauty

Over wine by the glass
"early bird" 20% off fine Italian dining
I reaffirmed my love of Russia
literate and subtle:
statues of poets in the parks
teen soldiers laughing on bus to work
detail, eyeing micro-minis
lipstick pouts and peroxide blonds,
embittered stares of old communists,
ethereal singing of boys in Pushkin Square
on his birthday June 6, 1997 as we arose
from beneath the streets
pilgrims released from marble halls
of Moscow Metro, dark Czech beer later
at Pasternak's *Propaganda* café,
where slender-hipped queens smoked
American cigarettes in corner booths;
my lover sleeping till eleven while I wrote
my impressions in a notebook.

ii. Nightblooming Flowers

Brought two pounds of coffee to Moscow
Wigstock the Movie, gifts for Andrei,
afternoons he steamed bitter milk for lattes
jet-lag banished to corners. His sister boiled
pelmini with salt, plates with sour cream and dill
Andrei watched me eat, happy. I could only say
"Spacibo" so many times,
Natasha waved them away. I bought drinks
at the gay bar, Three Monkeys, we stood circled
among Armani shirts, heavy wristwatches
and expensive foreign sneakers;
watched curious boys severe in drag
shape vowels with their contorted bodies
—nightblooming flowers beating time to Russian techno;
man pressed teen with tales of wealth;
would he give up washing dishes or hawking smokes
from roadside kiosks to make quick bucks
going with foreigners? —Finally drunk
we stumbled outside to curb, hired
passing car as taxi back
to concrete tombstone apartment blocks
driver studied Andrei's hand in mine
Kevin over-tipped.

iii. Hunger

After insulting her I vowed
never to speak for Russia again,
no sweeping statements
or self-righteous American critiques
—only specifics: the tiny boy in dirty sneakers
who watched Andrei at the kiosk
buying beer for our picnic, cautious approach
familiar resigned eyes. So scared.
"I'll sleep with you for bread."
One dollar equaled sixty five hundred rubles
then, a few hundred rubles to the boy
—pennies really, not enough
to keep him from asking another man, not enough
to look suspicious.
"Could be police trap."
was all Andrei would say, rushed
us away, past war widows begging
at Metro stops, New Russians
growling into cell phones
man in Mercedes peeling bananas
one after another, wolfing them down.

iv. Defiance

Moscow's eyes follow strangers, follow
foreigners stiffly descending slopes
kilometer long escalators, marble halls
into Metro cathedral. Children
scrutinize, head-to-toe, weigh
wealth in clothes, examine shoes, posture
faces around them. Streets filled
with passing eyes, scrutinized
lone black face bobbing in Slavic crowd,
migrant African labor from former
Soviet satellite, stared
dead ahead, neither right nor left
ignored the alien attention
fixed on him. Three months she refused
to speak to me
for making this observation. While I
surprised at how familiar Moscow's
streets of wary caution felt to me,
a privileged American, wary
of hungry men, of cruel and horny men
of further violence
—the defiance felt the same.

v. In Gorky's House

In Gorky's house we put slippers made of carpet
over our shoes, made whispered steps
across the parquet floors as we drank in
that jewel of art deco filigree sunk amidst
the sewer of Stalinist architecture of central Moscow.
The staircase banister was a pale green stone
carved in drips that poured from the upper floor,
the sumptuous library held rich chocolate leather chairs
to immerse oneself as one sinks into fine literature
and Gorky's writing room was spare, practical
as Spartan as his prose, and as hard-nosed.

vi. Reconstruction

This prison, once a monastery within the capital's center ring
high dense walls, barbed wire
used to retain political prisoners
till TB or hunger killed them
or a regime change set them free. By summer
1997 the Orthodox church controlled it again.
As we walked the narrow streets I imagined
monks with leather hands sprung from
Soviet work camps removing barbed wire, rolling
gigantic coils to be resold to protect mafia dachas,
all of Moscow was under renovation, stonecutters
with electric saws split enormous blocks
of white marble to restore the ancient façade of pride;
black-masked welders cutting steel high above
in sturdy skeletons of new office buildings, still at work
6 o'clock on a Saturday night, summer spent
racing against the coming snow; young soldiers
boyish and fierce guarded throughways, waved traffic
away, attentive eyes on us; crowds of workmen in tan
overalls, gray overalls walking to jobs, standing
in circles around open pits, taking turns
manually digging new sewer lines, flattening
the hollow filters of harsh Russian cigarettes,
exhaling black, sour smoke. Past the middle
school that resembled a factory we stopped
for dinner, early for the out-of-fashion
nightclub to open. Alone on the dance floor
we danced away, Andrei's arms
swung like a scarecrow, jerked like a puppet
laughing, his resentment forgotten
—I'd locked him out and fallen asleep one night
early in my trip while he negotiated
with his ex-girlfriend across town. Disoriented
by jet-lag I let the phone ring. From far away
a thrumming sound rapidly approached
accompanied by Andrei's anguished howl. Sleepy,
roused, unlocked the vinyl-padded apartment door
he rushed in and slammed it, panting
leaning against it as if to secure our refuge
from angry neighbors. Exhausted, I sank
into the kitchen booth while he yelled at me
convinced I no longer loved him. Finally
my tired begging won him over, his disposition
repaired, he took me to bed.

vii. Repose

In Red Square St. Vasily's church so glorious the Czar
had the architect blinded
so he could never create its rival. At the foot
of the Kremlin's red brick wall a two level
red marble step pyramid, like a small bunker
—immortal Lenin's tomb. In June 1997 the lines
to pay respect were gone, the honor guard, unpaid
gone home. A single soldier stood at the end
of the hall inside, closely scrutinized everyone
with complete command. In his glass coffin
Lenin reclined, tipped slightly, his translucent yellow
face raised with utopian dreams; not trusting
Stalin, not anticipating Brezhnev's clumsy stewardship
over the accelerating decay of the Soviet economy,
not expecting a communist, Gorbachev to end
Soviet rule or for a Yeltsin to dismantle seventy years
of struggle and give away the store. Andrei
pushed me. The guard was staring with menace. One
isn't allowed to pause and wonder why
Lenin's left hand rested flat on the Soviet banner
which covered his waist, or why his right hand was closed
in a pallid fist, as if a boxer in repose. A boy
wearing a baseball cap walked in and the guard barked
sharply. The kid whipped the hat off his head
blushing ferociously. Outside, Stalin decayed in the ground
thanks to Khrushchev, John Reed's ashes honored
by a plaque on the Kremlin wall —the only American
recognized by the Revolution. We went to McDonald's
for lunch, paid a fortune so Andrei could beam in pride
when I admitted it tasted exactly the same
as in America.

viii. Twilight

"Gay Beach" beside the Moscow River
was a long walk from the overpass, knee-high
grasses and clusters of teens sunning
with liters of pear flavored soda and picnics,
thin blond Russian youth that Andrei
scolded me for watching. I couldn't help myself
I wanted to see everything, every face—
the Armani shirts open to the waist on the young men
who stood in groups smoking Marlboros by the Metro
entrance, the little girls dressed like hookers
shocking to this mongrel puritan, and here
among the trees scattered men, attentive to passerby
a lingering smile, asking for a light, etc. In that strange twilight
of semi-secret gay life word of mouth
told you where to go and how long to look
before you smiled: lunch hours in park beside Chechovskya
Metro station, Bolshoi Theater by Stalin's statue
after a show, delicate boys who wanted to be
ballerinas made-up and worshipped
for athletic elegance, cruised; following a handsome face
rising on opposite escalator as Andrei
cupped my ass giggling; tight jeans and aerobic pants
on the hustlers in the Café Français, their smiling
triumphant pimp measuring my glance.

ix. Asylum

We caught the electrichka into the city center, then a bus
our tickets bit by metal teeth clamped to the wall
then dusty streets, broken sidewalks, overgrown weeds
past muddy courtyards and unhappy children
playing listlessly on Soviet playground toys
to the insane asylum where the project rented office space.
Andrei told me that dissidents and convicted homosexuals
were imprisoned there until Perestroika and decriminalization;
we made out everywhere in retaliation, on the stairs
in echoing mint green halls, our tender queer souls
overturning horrors of electroshock torture and drugs
which confused and murdered earlier generations of men
who happened to love the wrong way. I drank black tea
while Andrei collected his pay and answered email
from American foundations willing to support their work. Outside
an inmate methodically painted a park bench
emerald green. I wondered how many coats that bench wore
how many inmates had dressed it, and would they ever
go naked and free. I saw Andrei differently that day
fighting for women's rights, standing up to Russian
machismo, his frail frame attuned to suffering
the fire inside focused on driving the stone
of civilization a few meters further.

x. Luggage

Andrei teased me about my luggage, "Is it too much?"
I asked, suddenly frightened. Did it make me a target?
Expose me as a foreigner to be attacked
and robbed? Andrei grew angry. "We are a civilized country!"
I reminded him of the Mission streets
I called home, the gang violence, shoot-outs with police
the cabbies left for dead. I was paranoid
everywhere, not just in Moscow, a fact
which didn't impress him. He looked at me
like I was a coward. How could I tell him
the fear that milked my courage
was my father's legacy? I tried
and failed each time, trying to stem arguments
and *explain*. There were so many people
out that night, groups of young men
who watched us pass and gauged
their chances. We bought liters of beer
from a kiosk, some brandy, a soda can
of pre-mixed gin and tonic. We ate our pastries
and waited for the midnight train, staring
at the empty tracks. The arriving train was beautiful
red velvet curtains hung in cheery windows
a luxurious adventure ahead. I tried to imagine
what Petersburg would look like,
the world-famous Hermitage Museum,
the streets, harbor and canals
of Peter's capital. We picked bunks
and chatted with our cabin mates, a small-time
official who spoke with Andrei
and stared at me, a young engineer
who shyly conversed in English. When we finished
our drinks, we went to the dining car, Andrei
introduced me to caviar, we held hands
aware of the waiter's attention and professed
undying love. Petersburg would undermine
everything, stripping our love to the bare threads
that bound us; tension would play its awful chords
and one by one sever those connections.

xi. Irises

The square was enormous, partially encircled
by a curving wall of ministerial buildings, a high arch
led to the streets outside the imperial palace
which had become the Hermitage. Shattering loud
rock music echoed off the walls, the square filled
with teens playing an Adidas sponsored competition
called "Street Ball" —basketball with savvy marketing
campaign. There were clothes giveaways
and vulgar advertising banners where the Czar's army
had once paraded. With ads for American cigarettes
in the Metros and above the roundabout at the end
of Nevsky Prospekt, Russia was fully infected
by American companies out to make a buck.
On the modern art floor I watched the games
from a window, then turned to admire a Van Gogh
iris bush with winding path beside. I wanted
to cross the frame and find out where that path
led. The painting next to it was of prosperous
fields, a low wall standing before a town
with many cottages, each with dinner smoking
from their chimneys. It was hopeful and naive,
a picture of how things ought to be. I admired the irises,
Andrei disagreed. We argued about Picasso,
Andrei found him ugly, while I still possessed
a deep respect for his wandering, cryptic invention.
In a tiny back room hung a sterile Kandinsky
reminding me of my weak joke the night I met Andrei,
"Ya kandinsky" poorly translated as "I'm confused." Over curry
his friends had taught me a more useful Russian phrase,
Можно, только осторожно.
Be careful of erotic wishes, you may get what you ask for.

xii. Fish Fabrique

The staircase was unlit, there was no electricity, we walked
carefully, unsure of our destination. Fish Fabrique,
the underground St. Petersburg club someone had recommended
was on the top floor, exposed brick walls tagged
with neon graffiti, a makeshift bar with cardboard cases
of warm beer, a couple thousand rubles apiece. Cheap.
We sat at a table overlooking an overgrown courtyard, the window glass
long since destroyed. A young Russian next to us eavesdropped
but none of us said hello. Mutual loss.
We passed the afternoon drinking our bottled beers, speaking
occasionally, two plus weeks exclusively together
our company wearing each other thin. Though I loved him
more than anything
I could not leave the States to move to the former Soviet Union
and the regret
was tearing me apart. In that seedy, St. Petersburg club
I could neither tell him
or admit it to myself, Russia
would never be my home, despite how I loved her son.

xiii. Shelter

Protected by apartments on every side
small grassy square, round gunmetal turret
tore open the ground, community fallout shelter
renamed "Griboyedov". Narrow concrete stairs
descended into ground, buzzer pressed, waited
before painted steel door, square window
finally slid open, blunt eyes scrutinized
then challenged us with a price. Andrei
translated, I agreed. Bunker opened
to music, perfume, cigarette smoke,
money man, large room, elaborate paintings, neon
graffiti, various fabrics, rave banners
Kali and psychedelic paradise, spectacular
Russian electronica, men outfitted
like urban royalty of any city worldwide
—the best gear: hip sneakers, designer threads.
Straight couple necked on padded bench
absorbing ambiance of chill room, women
internationally sophisticated, deeply feminine
in short skirts, hip tops, dyed hair. Video montage
of Pushkin's bronze horseman, Petersburg streets
rows of New Russian shops, mesmerizing
intricate music. Congratulated filmmaker
with clockwork Russian, "Horrorshow!"
Andrei grimaced. We chatted in English,
went for more drinks. "Gin! Tonic!"
Bartender confused, then double charged.
Last few rubles gone, only two other gay men
—too pretty to approach. We held each other up
through unlit streets, when approached
Andrei reminded, "We're drunk and Georgian"
citing the only two occasions
when Russian men
could walk in each other's arms
excused and ignored.

xiv. Postcard Romance

I visit St. Petersburg again with you in my thoughts
the beautiful city which destroyed us
with its punishing long streets
and high prices. We lived off beer and blinis
fought bitterly over packs of cigarettes
and sought refuge from despair in Warhol's Frankenstein
badly dubbed into Russian.
Made dumb with exhaustion
knowing only the words for please and thank you
I rarely spoke in public
and kept my own counsel
trying to insulate you from my fear
of the chaos in your country
my distrust of the hardness of men
and my resentment at being dependent on you
feeling I couldn't say no
—caged by your desire.
I saved my pain for the goodbye letter
words hammered home in a list of grievances
which severed our bond like a rusted scythe
wounding us both.

xv. Stranded

Moon frosted fields fled past window
of my berth in the sleeping car
Andrei asleep below. Russia
grandly large, an expanse greater
than the American West, as yet untamed
or tragically polluted. From the tracks
came a long scream, unwinding as the train
hurried on toward Moscow, our Petersburg
née Leningrad trip finished in fights over money
and an afternoon tucked behind a storefront
movie house watching Warhol's *Frankenstein* in 3D
dubbed hilariously into Russian, wearing oversize
plastic glasses with scratched lenses, little boys
and old men watching the naked breasts on screen.
We'd been caught going into the National Gallery
to look at jars of pickled punks and photographs
of freaks; the woman collecting tickets took one look
and nailed me as a foreigner, trying to pay
the local's ticket price. She asked me something
I had no answer to, "Where do you live?" Caught between my love
and San Francisco. "Is he deaf too?" she asked. Embarrassed,
we skulked out, accompanied by her mocking laughter. Again
we paced Nevsky Prospekt, hung out in the park
with prostitutes and toughs under the overcast sky. Andrei smoked
refused my offer of coffee, angrily confessed
he was out of money. His salary was good for a Russian
but the train had cost him, his generosity in the dining car,
his refusal to accept a dime from me, the meals
the twin beds in our room —all expensive, and I
was ungrateful and afraid. We waited for the train
in silence, I had brought too much luggage —prepared
for anything except his growing resentment.
It was a relief to go aboard. I awoke late that night
as the train ground to a stop a long way from anywhere.

xvi. Scream

The American woman and her daughter were alone
touring Eastern Europe like the mystic Madame Blavatsky
using a card filled with cartoons to serve as translator.
"If we're hungry, we point to this." They seemed so naïve
and fearless, didn't they realize? Stranded, we shared our food
and promised to help them find the hostel
after we arrived in Moscow. In the night I had heard a scream
and thought of small-town kids saluting
the distant train with Baltika beer, vodka swigs
and bare asses. I wondered at how their voices followed
and faded as we hurtled down the tracks. It had been
the American woman instead. "I was sleeping and this man
fell on top of me. He was drunk. So I screamed.
He just sat there, staring at me. So I screamed again. Finally
he got up and climbed into his bunk. But I didn't sleep
the rest of the night." "Chechens." Andrei told me,
insinuating something distasteful and lazy. Three years later
the Red Army would invade Grozny again, on the pretense
of terrorist bombs in Moscow apartments. Vladimir Putin
would be a hero and in Moscow, silence
from the love that had written every day.

xvii. Babushka

Beyond us, down Soviet iron tracks
metal train cargo car twisted in half
obstructed our passage back
from St. Petersburg to Moscow
following another bitter fight.
Breakfast salami, black tea
warm fruit yogurt long ago finished
Andrei out of smokes
no food or alcohol in the dining car
no potable water except what we brought
the day proved wearying long.
We paced the tracks, gladly I spent
the four plus bucks for his cigarettes
Andrei gradually relaxed.
Smoking on the tracks, hefty peasant woman
in checkered headscarf led
an army of passengers towards the wreck.
We joked about the new revolutionary army
as a man returned with fried potatoes
he'd bought from a kindly Babushka
near where we'd stopped. My first look
into wooden peasant dacha from Russia's past
heavy wool richly patterned carpets
hung on the walls, Babushka had never
seen an American in person, never imagined
she'd have one in her house for fried potatoes
onions and homemade pickles from the fridge.
She took the handful of rubles Andrei offered
and gave him half back protesting
"No, it's too much money." Mother Russia
fussing over her queer sons.

xviii. Souvenirs

In a file folder with his hurt words
I found receipts from Russia, my itinerary
Finn Air San Francisco Helsinki Moscow
eight hundred one dollars so many hours
a tiny lock on my back pack, my luggage
broken in the cargo hold, tickets to the Hermitage,
St. Vasily's cathedral in Red Square, National Museum
we were banished from, the six thousand rubles
—approximately one US dollar summer 1997
that allowed me, an American, into the red brick walls
of Russia's restricted Kremlin, guard towers rising
like church steeples, serious men examining
our faces and clothes for sedition. Andrei embarrassed
about playing tourist in his hometown, while I
was doing it for my father the whole time
walking where Czars and premiers, where Stalin himself
had walked and ruled, crushed dissent
ended millions of lives. We entered the armory
filled with fantastic gifts to the family that ruled
most of Asia yet envied Europe. I remember
hammered silver chariot pulled by jewel-encrusted
elephant, fabergé eggs with delicate clockwork train
powered by gold key, tiny model of the Kremlin,
riches too varied and extraordinary to describe
—my beloved intelligentsia was unimpressed
by such tacky wealth. Outside, manicured
lawns and roses, a mighty bell —the largest
ever cast, forged of children's pennies, church relics
gone to foundry, an enormous wedge of bronze
broken like a smashed dinner plate
while it cooled. I see it again in photos
from Internet porn sites, young male models posing
before it with nervous smiles, thumbs hooked casually
in their belts. I have no other photographs
of Russia, my camera sat in my bag, too afraid
to stand out as tourist, too entranced
to steal a single moment from immediate experience
and spend it recording, too in love, amazed
to be in Russia across divide of politics, homophobia
and the vulgar violence we had both survived.

xix. Trust

Beside the train platform small stores
in pre-fab rectangular buildings contained
a single long counter with rows of vodka
and soft drinks, or freezer cases with pelmini
crowded with boxes of foreign fruit juice. Outside
old women sold loaves of homemade bread
dried fish and toilet paper. I gave
one babushka a 10,000 ruble note
and watched her as she counted my change.
She paused, seeing if she could cheat me, I continued
to stare, and she counted out a few more bills, then swore
as I continued to scrutinize her. In the pre-fab
liquor store I asked for "Krystal" not knowing
every vodka was "Krystal". I bought tonic too
but in my rush to return to angry Andrei
and speak English again I forgot it on the counter.
I was learning to read Cyrillic, but knew few words
relying entirely on Andrei for translating, for ordering
lunch, navigating the subway, buying antihistamines
when my allergies slew me. He could see
I was afraid, how I hung back and rarely spoke
in public, and he despised me. After arguing
about my lack of compassion following a difficult meeting
with his ex-girlfriend, hoping to placate I asked Andrei
if I could buy him cigarettes. He pointed to the window
hung back, waiting for my humiliation. I asked for cigarettes,
the clerk demanded what brand, what color,
and I was at sea, unable to respond.
I looked to Andrei helplessly, noting his triumph
he stepped forward and completed the transaction
breaking my heart. As much as I loved him
I would never trust him again
and did not know how to forgive this.

xx. Table Manners

The kitten I was allergic to danced in time
to teasing string, Andrei's broad-shouldered
mother bustled in, loaded with groceries
and his step-father, the military man
grinned and shook my hand vigorously
to show we were all friends now. Andrei's mother
shooed him from the kitchen, sending him
on an errand to fetch ice cream for the boys. Andrei
smiled at me, embarrassed, seeing his mother's wide
peasant biceps and coarse commands
to her husband. I liked her immediately. Without warning
plate after plate of food was set on the table
pelmini, meats, thick black bread, soft white cheese
more food than I'd seen that entire trip. I waited
for her to join us, looking at Andrei for confirmation.
"Eat! Eat!" She slapped the table loudly with both palms
the words understood though beyond my meager Russian.
Andrei grinned at me, every time a plate was put down
I murmured "Spacibo" and she "Pajalusta." Andrei
in stitches as his mother remarked at how polite I was
and how much I could put away. His stepfather came in
with loud greetings and was scolded by mother
who reached for groceries and slapped his hands away
from the table where we were eating. He retreated to the bedroom
to television and a bottle, occasionally describing his shows
from the other room. "Idiot!" Andrei's mother exclaimed.
We looked at each other giggling. We would be arguing in an hour
as we always did, just prior to separation. Andrei
had hired a twenty dollar taxi to take me to the airport
the next morning, a white Mercedes, it seemed too luxurious
too pricey. We slept together in the living room
his mother shrugging at the accommodations, thinking nothing
unusual. I awoke wondering why the alarm
hadn't rung. Andrei hadn't set it and we were late. I panicked
about losing the taxi, about missing my flight.
Amused, Andrei herded me out the door and down
the dark elevator, the driver put his cel phone in his pocket
and halfway to the airport I paid him. The busy departure hall
filled with Indians, Chinese, Europeans and Russians
all leaving. In line Andrei refused the seventy dollars in rubles
I had left, "It's illegal to take them out," I protested. He smiled
defying me. I couldn't understand why. He was broke

and they were useless to me in the States. Too sleepy to suggest
he change them for me, the line swept me past the security gates
and Andrei beyond reach, looking at me with pity
—suddenly lost and alone in the bustling station, wanting
a hug goodbye and scolded by passport control. As I turned
Andrei fled the scene, relieved no doubt
to be rid of me.

xxi. Shedding Skins

In midnight's bed I practice testimony to Andrei's advocate
who scolded me once with biblical love. I have seen
Hell, been stripped of skin and flesh,
restrung thread by thread
these jangling nerves, knit muscle fibers to bone
plastered this nervous, pock-marked skin
over the seething memories. No longer
in trance-state, no longer
hearing voices of some random dialed radio
sifting the loose phrases for directions
out of that geography of grief
we fought all the time, drinking nights
to halt our disputes, romantics though I knew
he would not accompany me through the grace
of my innocence, would not hold me
lost to terror, would only smile
when I woke screaming, and could not see
the blood on my face, my fingers
in my eyes, but he would destroy me
hostage to his pleasure, responsible
for his smile. Only alone could I descend
skin bubbling with pustules, trembling
at consummation, at his hungry touch
clothes shed in bonfires, skins shed
again to the meat of darkness, of fears
remembering how I loved a man as a child
and he split me open like a memory
turning me inside out, all nerves
and fright, lost in a horror of silence
because the squeaky wheel got hit
not knowing silence too was fist
that locked the scream
inside, amplifying anger
until a blood sacrifice was required
to stifle the whimpering in my bed.

xxii. Additive Freedom

He flattened the hollow cardboard "filter" of the Beliemorkanal cigarette,
laughing
"I usually do not smoke such trash," But Tom insisted I try
one of those strange Soviet smokes, the tobacco rolled like shotgun pellets
bitter sandpaper inside my throat. I looked from him to Tom
and Tom exclaimed, "It was all there was
when I visited Volodya in Petersburg."
We knew that scene, lovers
separated by continents, but I
didn't have the stomach any more for this tragic love affair
rarely consummated. I drank my white wine,
fished an American Spirit out of my pocket
and lit it. The smoke was additive free, and the next day
it was over.

xxiii. Dyusha

With Dyusha's death onstage at 43
a piece of our time together erodes
and I'm left with soft edges: of coffees
at the radical Moscow art museum with you
Dyusha and his manager who looked down at us
until she heard I was American and that Dyusha
had sat in a kitchen in San Francisco and played
an acoustic guitar, singing quietly to us in Russian.
I remember your eyes afire and Tom saying,
You don't know how special this is.
But I did. I knew that Andrei "Dyusha" Romanov
had played in Akvarium, Russia's Beatles
(as Tom said) and had switched from piano to flute
following Ian Anderson's lead;
I knew the voice of resistance could overcome political oppression,
his censored band having spread by cassette tape
recorded in apartment "studios" because Melodia
(the Soviet label) wouldn't record them;
and I saw it in your eyes, drinking red wine
not vodka, around a table side-by-side with liberty's soldier
a bearded man with smiling eyes
who played despite censors, poverty or police
until last Thursday, when he died onstage
ten years into democracy. These soft edges
sharpen with conviction: I distinctly choose to remember.

xxiv. Late Summer / Fall

After four year's silence I saw Andrei
walking up Church Street past the Pilsner Inn.
Time stopped, I grew dizzy, we talked. At dinner
he told me that sushi is all the rage in Moscow
even Italian restaurants serve it. I remembered
strips of dried, salted fish Andrei peeled and fed me
over Baltika No. 4 beer. "You can get anything
in Moscow." At his new boyfriend's apartment
we watched a Chekhov film about ex-lovers
reunited, and their crushed expectations. Andrei got drunk
on Jose Cuervo and bitter Chinese vodka, asking again
why did I break up with him. I made excuses
like before, that I wasn't ready, stress of separation.
How could I tell him that I saw our future
in his joking quotes from "Who's Afraid
of Virginia Wolfe"? That staying with me
I imagined him self-destruct through drinking
destroying me along the way? The signs
were too frequent to ignore, how Andrei called me
whore, the constant fights, how he drank
just to tolerate my company. I loved Andrei too much
to watch that great man disintegrate, and knew
I would be blamed for his fall.

xxv. Epilogue

Hearing his voice hesitate, returning my call
a week later, something turns within me
I remember the way he twisted my ring
from his finger, the line of his mouth
accepting what he could not understand
and I could not explain. Rising past our sorrow
years softening coarse edges
of real and imagined slights, fonder memories:
how we took the electrichka to his apartment
bought cheese and bread, steamed milk
discovered his sister's forgotten teenage makeup
and became glorious, ever more beautiful, his goatee
smiling with lipstick, his pale eyes framed
in mascara and eye shadow. I went 80's
New Wave wreckage with heavy blue lines
and *Blade Runner* eyes. He put on Natasha's
fur hat and Vogued Russian-style. My arms wrapped
around his waist, kissing his neck from behind;
we slow danced like middle school kids
then made out like teens in fulfillment
of too many lonely years, of those plaintive conversations
I shared with no one when I wanted to die. His voice,
surprised smile through a window, recognition
in my instinctive embrace —all symptoms of hope
in some future where we converge, when he grasps
the nature of my terror and finally respects
how sometimes it hurts to be touched, not for lack of love
but because of a seizure of historic fear that gloves my heart
dulls my eyes and mind, banishes me to a distance
that can only be bridged by patient kindness
and the casual insistence of compassion.

About The Author

W.R. Taylor is a twelve year veteran of San Francisco. He has watched his friends cut themselves bellowing for justice, miss their psyche meds and be swallowed whole. He has lost friends to AIDS, heroin, mental illness, prostitution, high rents, and the passage of time. He is a survivor of sexual assault, sexual bliss, sexual confusion, and manic euphoria.

A San Francisco trained social activist, Taylor understands the personal is political, recognizing the link between the arts and social change. Consequently, he has written and published about childhood sexual abuse, queer and gender identity, prostitution, fringe and drug culture, HIV/AIDS, mental health disabilities, metaphysics, philosophy and art.

Taylor is the author of *Chiseled Orchids* published by New Athens Press. His work has been featured in *The James White Review, Suspect Thoughts, Velvet Mafia, Other Magazine, Prosodia,* and UK based *The International Journal of Erotica.*

Despite our difficult historical moment, he is filled with hope for the future.

www.ingramcontent.com/pod-product-compliance
Lightning Source LLC
Chambersburg PA
CBHW020343290526
45785CB00005B/2156